Samuel de Champlain

Dedicated to our teachers,
Lorraine and Bud Dilling

Betty Sherwood and Janet Snider

canchron books
Canadian Chronicles
Toronto, Canada

Acknowledgements

We wish to thank the following people for their support and assistance during the adventure of creating this book: James Casquenette, Scott Bradford, Jacqueline Snider, Benoit Clermont, Nancy Golden, Jill Solnicki, Laura Cairns, Ed and Myrna Levy, Jacques and Lise Clermont, Paula Dotey, Rachelle Richard, Isabella McConkey, Monique Van Remortel, David Gilmour, Bill Moore, Dr. Lita-Rose Betcherman, Christine Bourolias, Rachel and Ryan Burns, Louis Campeau, Nicole Chamberland, Kenneth Crooke, Sandra Diamant-Ross, Susan Danforth, Robert Gosselin, Tara Haggar, Bob and Sheila Henderson, Mary Beth McCleary, Sheila Moll, Stefanie Moy, Karen Pearce, Diane Reed, Pat Steenbergen, Sherry Stewart, Dorathy Thiakos, and Henry Yee.

Canadian Cataloguing in Publication Data

Sherwood, Betty, 1943-
    Samuel de Champlain

(Explorer Chronicles ; 1)
Includes bibliographical references and index
ISBN 0-9688049-0-X

1. Champlain, Samuel de, 1567-1635 - Juvenile literature. 2. New France - Discovery and exploration - French - Juvenile literature. 3. Canada - History - To 1663 (New France) - Juvenile literature* 4. Explorers - Canada - Biography - Juvenile literature. I. Snider, Janet, 1944- . II. Title. III. Series.

FC332.S53 2001   j971.01'13'092   C00-932816-5
F1030.1.S53 2001

Print Production by LithArt.com
Toronto, Canada

Contents

Samuel de Champlain   page 4

Voyage to the St. Lawrence - 1603   page 9

Port Royal - 1605   page 13

Québec - 1608   page 18

Did You Know?   page 20

Champlain's Map - 1632   page 21

Travels to Lake Huron - 1615   page 27

Conclusion   page 35

Glossary   page 36

More To Do   page 37

Bibliography/Picture Credits   page 39

Index   page 40

Samuel de Champlain (1567-1635)

"After the Edict of Nantes in 1598, France had a rest from foreign and civil strife, so could turn again to exploration. Champlain gave the best years of his life, always travelling with a hungry heart, with the Great South Sea ever a day's journey in advance." W. L. Grant, Professor of Colonial History, Queen's University, Kingston, 1906.

Champlain

As I look back on my life, the voyages I undertook to find and settle New France for our king fill me with pride and wonder. I marvel at the new lands I saw, the Native people I met, many of whom became friends and the strength and the courage of the settlers in New France.

I grew up in Brouage, a coastal town on the Bay of Biscay. Ships and the sea were ever-present and I was entranced with them at an early age. I learned to read and write at home and had a predisposition to drawing. These early experiences stood me in good stead for my future life of exploring, map-making and writing.

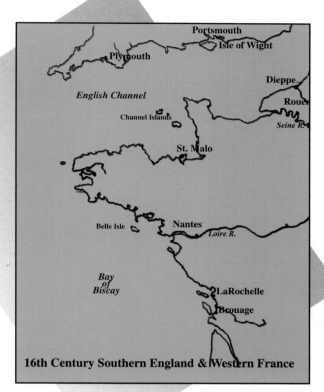

16th Century Southern England & Western France

I had been a quarter-master in the king's army in Brittany during the religious wars, but after the Treaty of Vervins in 1598 that settled the differences between France and Spain, I found that I had no occupation. With nothing to do, the sea beckoned me. I went to Spain, where my uncle Provençal, a ship's captain, had been appointed chief pilot to the King of Spain. There was news of the English attacking Porto Rico. The king gathered an army together of twenty ships to set sail for the Indies.

Champlain's Birthplace

Brouage was on the Bay of Biscay when Champlain was a boy. Now it lies 3 kilometres inland. Brouage imported Dutch settlers to reclaim the salt marshes around it in the seventeenth century.

After some changes in plans, I finally realized my ambition to sail to the New World as captain of the "St. Julien," my uncle's ship. We set sail in January 1599.

Our first port-of-call was Guadeloupe. I had my first taste of fresh West Indian fruit. How good it all tasted. There was a pearl fishery off Margarita Island where Negro slaves, in the service of the King of Spain, dove in sixty or seventy feet of water and gathered shellfish in a basket. The shellfish looked very much like our oysters. Their catch was turned over to the king's officers.

By the time we arrived in Porto Rico it had been attacked and was in ruins. The King of Spain had sent the garrison (all the soldiers) to Cartagena [in Colombia] to ward off an attack there, so there were no soldiers in Porto Rico to resist attack by the British. The people were happy to see us and made us welcome. They had plantain and oranges and many other fruits I had not seen or eaten before. They also had a small parrot-like bird which they called a parakeet. The Natives would teach them to talk.

Before leaving Porto Rico, the General divided the fleet into three groups. I was one of the group that went to New Spain [Mexico]. On the way, we chased some British ships because foreigners were not permitted to trade in these waters.

Trade in Cacao (Hot Chocolate)

In 1519, Hernando Cortez brought hot chocolate to Europe where it was enjoyed by the nobility. Champlain described the native recipe: the fruit was powdered, made into a paste, steeped in hot water, then honey and spice were added. All were boiled together and drunk warm in the morning. Today, the average American eats 5.4 kg. (12lb.) of chocolate per year.

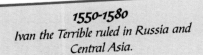

1550-1580
Ivan the Terrible ruled in Russia and Central Asia.

1564-1616
William Shakespeare

1565
The first pencil with graphite lead and a wooden cover was designed in Switzerland.

During the chase a funny thing happened. It came about like this: a pinnace appeared without warning among our ships. We hailed her crew repeatedly. When they made no reply we opened fire, but the pinnace continued to run before the wind. Our men were afraid to board because they could see nobody at the helm. They thought she was being steered by the devil. Finally we got a boarding party on the pinnace but it was empty. When the others heard how the soldiers had been afraid to board an empty ship we all had a good laugh at their expense.

When we landed at San Juan [Mexico], I was given permission to travel to Mexico City,

three hundred miles inland. I was astonished at the magnificent temples, palaces and great houses, the broad avenues and handsome shops stocked with goods of all kinds. When the Spanish conquerors first arrived, the Native population in Mexico was treated very badly. The Natives worship the moon and pray to it for power.

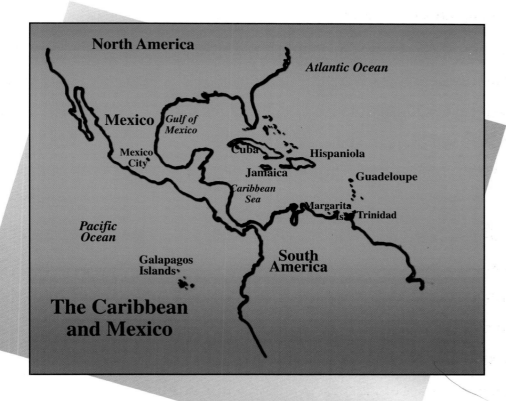

The Caribbean and Mexico

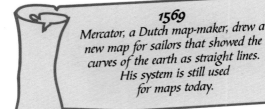

1569
Mercator, a Dutch map-maker, drew a new map for sailors that showed the curves of the earth as straight lines. His system is still used for maps today.

1560-1570
The Iroquois Confederacy formed consisting of: Seneca, Oneida, Onondaga, Cayuga and Mohawk nations. (total population 30,000)

1570
First atlas made by Abraham Ortelius in Belgium

Right at the outset, the King of Spain established the Inquisition. There were so many Natives condemned to slavery or death that the very telling of it brings tears to my eyes. It was mistreatment of this sort that drove the Natives, in desperation, to the mountains where they seized and ate as many Spaniards as they could find. Eventually, the Spanish were compelled to withdraw the Inquisition and to allow the Natives liberty with regard to their beliefs and governed them more leniently.

Before sailing back to Europe, I also spent time in Cuba. Havana had the best harbour that I saw in the Indies. The island was mountainous so they didn't grow corn or vines, but they grew a delicious fruit called pineapple. It has a pleasant taste, as sweet as sugar. On leaving Cuba, we set sail for Spain and arrived after an absence of two years and two months.

The Inquisitors at Work in Mexico
(Champlain's voyage 1599-1601)

My first experience of the New World gave me knowledge that I used effectively in my explorations of New France: the myriad variety of nature, both animals and plants; an introduction to the Native population and their different customs; and my continued desire to find a northern route to the Orient.

Voyage to the St. Lawrence-1603

My second voyage was for the King of France in 1603. I set sail on the "Bonne Renommée" with my good friend François Pont-Gravé following in his ship. Our objective was fur trading along the St. Lawrence River, but what sticks in my mind are the encounters with the Natives.

When we reached Tadoussac, the first fur trading post in New France at the mouth of the Saguenay River, about one hundred Montagnais were engaged in a tabagie (feast) with their sagamo (chief), named Anadabijou. He welcomed Pont-Gravé and me after the fashion of the country and made us sit on either side of him. We brought two Natives to act as interpreters

who had been with us in France during the previous year. One spoke and told the party assembled that he had been received by King Henri and he felt sure that His

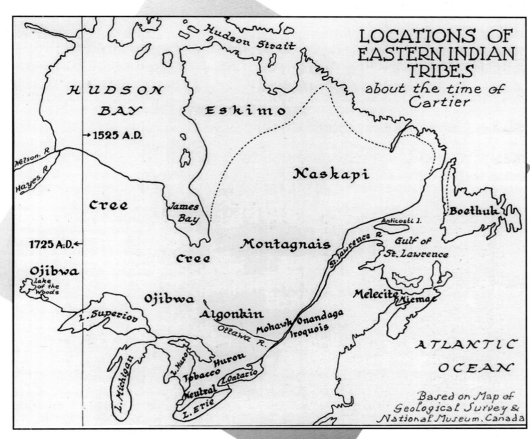

Majesty wished their people well and wanted only to settle the country and bring their enemies, the Iroquois, to a peaceful agreement or to conquer them. He also talked of the great houses and palaces, the fine people and their manner of living. He described our carriages as boxes pulled by moose because the Montagnais had no experience of horses or of wheels. The Natives listened in complete silence, then the Sagamo began to smoke his pipe. He passed it to Pont-Gravé and me in turn and then to the other chiefs. After this, he spoke in a solemn voice about His Majesty being a friend and all the party cried out in one voice, "Ho, ho, ho," which means yes, yes, yes.

They eat moose (which tastes like beef), bear, seal, beaver and many kinds of fowl. In the middle of the lodge they had eight or ten kettles full of meat, each on its own fire.

They used bowls made of bark, ate with their fingers and wiped the grease on their hair or on their dogs. They did not have table manners such as we had learned in France. They danced, a couple of men sang and the others kept time by clapping. Every so often they cried, "Ho, ho, ho!" This was a celebration of victory by three nations, the Etchimins, Algonquins and the Montagnais over Iroquois who they had surprised at the mouth of the Richelieu River. They have to rely on surprise because they are outnumbered by the Iroquois.

The next day, the Montagnais moved their camp from St. Matthew's Point to the waterfront at Tadoussac, next to our ship. At sunup, the grand Sagamo had gotten up and gone from lodge to lodge, crying out in a loud voice that they should break camp and move to Tadoussac to be close to

1571-1603
Idris Alooma, king of the largest trading empire in central Africa

1576-1578
Sir Martin Frobisher's three Arctic voyages

1578
Sir Francis Drake sailed to the coast of California and claimed it for England, in his circumnavigation of the world

their friends. It certainly didn't take them long to accomplish this. The chief launched his canoe carrying his wife and children and a quantity of furs, followed by two hundred others. The canoes were remarkably fast considering that they were only paddled by a man and a woman. Our shallop was well-manned but we could not keep up to their speed. Their birchbark canoes were the most wonderful invention for travelling in this country because of their weight: they are so light, a man can carry his own canoe and yet it will transport up to a thousand pounds.

After being at Tadoussac for some time, we set off up river to explore and to map the coast with our destination being Montréal. Along the way we encountered rapids. In one place we couldn't continue with the ship, so Pont-Gravé and I got in our skiff that had been built specifically to run the rapids. Several Natives in their canoes showed us the way. We had hardly gone three hundred yards before the men had to get out and haul the skiff along. The Natives, though, had no such problems and were able to paddle their canoes with no trouble. I realized that if I were ever going to map this country, find the Great Salt Sea they talk of and look for a passage to the Orient, I would have to travel, like the Natives do, by canoe.

Montagnais hunting Moose in Winter

1585
Sir Walter Raleigh explored Virginia.

1588
The Spanish armada was defeated by the British navy.

1590
The dome of St. Peter's Cathedral was completed in Rome.

The lands that we explored were fertile, covered with trees, including: hazelnut, chestnut, cherry, and fruit-bearing bushes such as: gooseberry, black and red currant, raspberries, strawberries and grapes. It was my opinion that the land around Trois Rivières would make an ideal place for a settlement. It could easily be fortified to help protect the tribes that trade with France but are hesitant to use the St. Lawrence River for fear of the Iroquois, their sworn enemies, who hold both sides of the river. With such a settlement, New France could gain control of both sides of the river.

On our way back to France that year, we stopped to see the copper mines near the Minas Basin [Nova Scotia]. There, the Natives told me a strange story about a terrible monster called Gongon, who lives on an island in Chaleur Bay. They said that the monster has the body of a woman but is ugly and so huge that one of our ship's masts would hardly come up to her waist. She eats people and keeps her victims in her great pocket until she is hungry. Some of them escaped and reported that her pocket is large enough to hold a ship. Apparently, the monster makes frightful hissing noises. When they were telling me all this they were terrified. All the Natives told me the same story, so I think a devil lives on that island and torments these poor people.

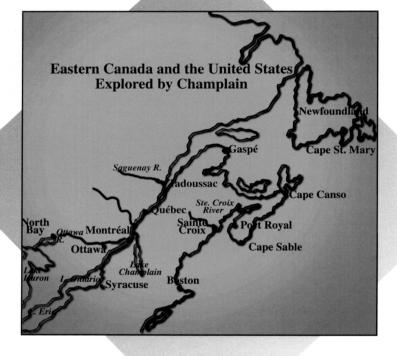

Eastern Canada and the United States Explored by Champlain

Newfoundland

Gaspé

Cape St. Mary

Saguenay R.

Tadoussac

Cape Canso

Ste. Croix River

Québec

North Bay

Ottawa R.

Montréal

Sainte Croix

Port Royal

Ottawa

Cape Sable

Lake Huron

Lake Champlain

L. Ontario

Syracuse

Boston

L. Erie

Port Royal-1605

Throughout all my voyages, it was my desire to settle New France. Our first successful settlement was at Port Royal [Nova Scotia] in 1605. On two ships we brought 120 colonists consisting of: workmen, masons, soldiers, surgeons, a pharmacist (Louis Hébert), a lawyer (Marc Lescarbot), an interpreter (Mathew D'Acosta), a Roman Catholic priest and a Huguenot minister. My friend, Pont-Gravé, Sieur de Monts (who was given the fur monopoly by King Henri), and the leader of the expedition, Jean de Biencourt, Seigneur de Poutrincourt arrived along with two fur trading vessels and a whaling ship. We moved the original Habitation from Ste. Croix [New Brunswick], where we had spent a disastrous winter marooned on an island with no access to wood or fresh water the previous year. Port Royal was a more sheltered site with a natural harbour [Annapolis Basin]. It was protected from the prevailing winds and weather by a line

Champlain's Drawing of Port Royal

of hills. There was fresh water and good soil. When we reconstructed the buildings we made them more compact to afford protection from the winds and attack. Lescarbot, a lawyer from Paris, was left in charge while Pont-Gravé, Poutrincourt, and I sailed south to explore the coast. Our explorations were fraught with many difficulties with both the ship and the crew. We returned to Port Royal in November of 1606 with heavy hearts. The spectacle that we saw when we anchored and lowered the long boat in the harbour erased all the bad memories of our recent trip.

Champlain supervises the building of the Habitation at Port Royal, 1605.

1600
In France 25% of winegrowers and 60% of independent farmers (middle class) could sign their names.

Early 1600's
In France all classes concerned with the cold. Lower classes feared hunger and disease. 50% of children did not reach adulthood. Plagues in French cities from 1399-1597

1603
Queen Elizabeth I died after reigning for 45 years.

The Habitation at Port Royal was reconstructed by the Canadian Government in 1938-39.

Port Royal

Port Royal was located where the village of Lower Granville is now. C. W. Jefferys, who was present at the excavation of the original site, describes it as follows: "The soil was carefully excavated and the foundation stones of the buildings were discovered... A well was found in the middle of the courtyard with many of its stones still in position. Every detail of construction was carefully worked out in accordance with the building methods and the style of the period. The massive chimneys were built of local stone, the fireplaces lined with brick made from the nearby clay pits from which Poutrincourt made bricks 390 years ago. All the beams, planks and shingles were hewn or sawn by hand, the nails and other iron works all hand wrought." The reconstruction of Port Royal is open to visitors in Nova Scotia.

We were greeted by King Neptune, whose boat was draped in the sea-god's colours, as a blue veil fluttered around him. His long silver hair and silver beard were made of seaweed and he wore tall boots and carried a trident. His vessel drew alongside our longboat and he spoke in a deep sonorous voice:

Halt mighty Sagamo, no further fare!
Look on a god who holds thee in his care.
Thou knows't me not? I am of Saturn's line
Brother to Pluto dark and Jove divine.

If man would taste the space of fortune's savour
He needs must seek the aid of Neptune's favour
For stay-at-homes who doze on kitchen settles
Earn no more glory than their pots and kettles.

1605
The Gunpowder Plot. Catholics conspired to blow up the English king and parliament. Guy Fawkes Day is still celebrated today with fireworks.

1605
"King Neptune" was the first play staged in Canada at Port Royal in November.

1605
"King Lear" first staged in England on Dec. 26

"King Neptune" was the first play staged in New France.

Mathew D'Acosta

D'Acosta was a black Portuguese man who was hired to be an interpreter of the Mi'kmaq language for three years at Port Royal and other parts of Acadia. His work was highly valued judging from his salary which was 180 livres per year. For comparison Louis Hébert, the pharmacist, was paid 100 livres per year. D'Acosta was the first black man in Nova Scotia and a member of the "Order of Good Cheer."

The brave souls toiling at Port Royal were happy to welcome us back and we were relieved and very happy to be home. That winter we kept up our spirits by instituting the "Order of Good Cheer" (Ordre de Bon Temps). During two winters in Acadia I had noticed that the active men were less likely to develop scurvy and thus survive the winter. Each gentleman at Poutrincourt's table spent two days before his turn as chief steward, hunting, fishing and preparing a hearty meal for all assembled. Naturally, competition set in so each chief steward tried to outdo the culinary delights of the one before. The evenings ended with a toast to the new chief steward when the chain of office was passed on, followed by the singing of folk songs. Twenty or thirty Mi'kmaqs regularly joined us in our banquets. We offered them bread, which they did not know how to make themselves. Memberton, their sagamo, joined us as an equal.

He told Poutrincourt that the French wine helped him sleep more soundly at night because it took away his fears.

Our relationship with the Mi'kmaqs was cordial. Some of them visited our Habitation almost every day. Memberton was king of his people and as such considered himself an equal to King Henri of France. We had the habit of greeting visiting French captains with a cannon salute. When Memberton returned to Port Royal after an expedition, he expected the same ceremonial greeting. Of course, we saluted him with the cannon too. He was the chief, but also the medicine man or shaman, a man greatly feared but greatly respected.

In the summer of 1607, after a successful winter in which all survived, with crops in the ground and flourishing, we had to quit Port Royal and return to France. Unfortunately, the exclusive rights to the fur trade enjoyed by our benefactor, de Monts, had been withdrawn by the king. There was no more money to maintain the Habitation and its workers. I never saw Port Royal again, but left it to Poutrincourt to continue the settlement there in later years.

Marc Lescarbot

Lescarbot was a Parisian lawyer who came to Port Royal with Champlain and was instrumental in establishing the "Order of Good Cheer" along with Champlain. He was a poet, dramatist and general morale booster for the workers and artisans who had left the familiarity of France for adventure and hardship at Port Royal. He staged the very first play to be performed in Nova Scotia. The famous Neptune Theatre in Halifax is named for that play.

He respected, liked and was tolerant of the Mi'kmaqs who lived around Port Royal. He praised their physical fitness, swiftness, keen-sightedness, and skill in hunting. He made some very interesting observations about the Mi'kmaqs in comparison to the French. He thought that they were morally laudable because of their courage, generosity and kindness to the members of their tribe. They were free from ambition, vainglory, envy and avarice (greed). They were very different from the French, who were competitive and quarrelsome. Lescarbot thought that the Mi'kmaq existence would be more secure if they settled in a fixed spot and planted crops, but they were too used to a nomadic life to change. He was shocked by their cruel justice to a woman traitor, but later he said, "This is their form of justice." No doubt he had in mind the rack and other devices of torture used in France at the time.

Québec City - 1608

The settlement of Québec was made possible when Henri the Great (Henri IV) gave exclusive fur trading rights to Sieur de Monts again. This enabled him to outfit our ships, purchase the materials and hire the artisans to build the Habitation. I was overjoyed at the thought of going back to this fertile land thriving with fruit and nut trees, forests and wildlife on the shores of the great river, St. Lawrence.

I chose the site on the point of Québec (Native for the narrows) which was covered with butternut trees. The workmen cleared the land and the carpenters erected the storehouse first, followed by the Habitation itself. All the way around our buildings I had a gallery made outside the second storey, which was a very convenient thing. By the beginning of September the gardens were flourishing and it looked altogether agreeable. [The site is in the Lower Town between Place-Royale and rue Notre Dame and the river]

Shortly after arriving I learned of a conspiracy to kill me from Antoine Natal. He had thought better of his involvement so divulged the plot led by Jean Duval, a locksmith in the settlement. They intended to turn over Québec to Basque (part of Spain) traders. All the conspirators were

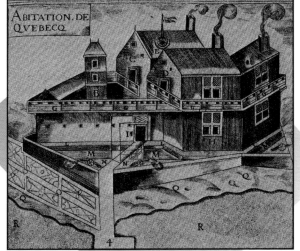

The Habitation at Québec was built in 1608, by Champlain's 28 member wintering party, below the cliffs that define present-day Québec City. It would be 25 years before a real town grew up around its site.

1606-1669
Rembrandt van Rijn, one of the world's greatest painters

1607
The Italians were the first to use forks.

1607-10
Henry Hudson's voyages into Hudson Bay

tried by a tribunal which included Pont-Gravé, the ship's captain, several of the officers and myself. Duval was sentenced to death by hanging and the other three conspirators were sent back to France with Pont-Gravé later in the year.

Eglise Notre-Dame-des-Victoires

The moat ditches of the Habitation run deep under this church and beneath the adjacent market square in the present Lower Town.

The whole time the Natives were with us, which was the safest place for them, they were in such constant dread of their enemies that they often took fright at night in their dreams and would send their wives and children to our fort. I used to keep the gates open for them, but insisted that the men remain outside the fort, for they were as safe there as if they had been inside.

I used to send out five or six men to give them courage by searching the woods to see if there was anything there. This would satisfy them. They were very timid and feared their enemies greatly, and hardly ever slept quietly wherever they were, although I reassured them everyday. I advised them to do the same as we did, that is to say, some of them would watch, whilst the others slept, and that each should have arms ready like a sentinel on duty. They used to say that we knew better than they did how to protect ourselves and that in time, if we were to come and live in their country, they would be able to learn our methods.

1608
John Smith saved by Pocahontas

1609
"Three Blind Mice" was written by Thomas Ravenscroft in England.

1609
Johan Kepler believed that the sun, not the earth, was the centre of the universe. He proved that the planets travelled around the sun in ellipses.

Did you know?

There is no known likeness of Champlain. The portrait is just this artist's idea.

The Champlain Sea was a body of salty water that extended from Québec City to Cornwall, Ontario and up the Ottawa Valley in prehistoric times, almost 13,000 years ago. It was named by American geologist C.H. Hitchcock in 1906. When properly drained, the marine clays left behind when the sea receded 10,000 years ago constitute the best agricultural land in Québec.

These streets and the Lower Town in Québec are named after Champlain.

Cochineal (Scarlet Dye)

This dye was a most important export from the New World, second only to silver and gold in value. Dyes were expensive, so coloured clothing had become a symbol of wealth. Peasants wore clothing made of homespun fabrics in shades of gray and light brown. Cochineal was used for dyeing wool, silk, Morocco leather, artist's paint and maraschino cherries.

The red dye was made in Mexico from the dried bodies of a female insect raised on the Indian fig plant . The Spanish forbade the export of the insects to maintain their monopoly. False rumours abounded about the source of the dye. Even Champlain was fooled when he described a field of cochineal in his Mexico journal.

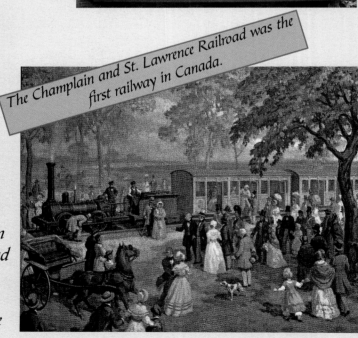

The Champlain and St. Lawrence Railroad was the first railway in Canada.

Champlain might have seen the first RV. When he was in Mexico, he saw Native people who had vans covered with bark and pulled by horses, mules or oxen. Wives and children lived in the vans while they stayed in one place for a couple of months and then moved on.

Champlain's Map - 1632

The winter in Québec was trying. Scurvy attacked several men and even some of the Natives. One day Natives appeared across the river shouting to us for aid. We could do nothing because of the ice. They got into their canoes and tried to cross the water between the ice floes but the canoes were crushed into a thousand pieces. They jumped onto a large block of ice which floated to our side of the river. It struck the shore so hard that they were thrown off upon the land. They came to our settlement so thin and emaciated that they looked like skeletons.

I was astonished at their appearance and at the way they crossed the river. If the Montagnais would take the trouble to sow Indian corn as do their neighbours, the Algonquins, Hurons and Iroquois, they would also be free from such cruel attacks of famine because they would know how to ward them off by care and foresight.

This is the artist's impression of Champlain travelling with Montagnais during his trip to Tadoussac in 1603.

The Habitation at Québec

Scurvy

These were the symptoms listed by Champlain: teeth fell out, gums bled, bodies got swollen with spots on them like flea bites, pain in arms and legs prevented walking. 35 out of 79 died at St. Croix and 20 were close to death when spring arrived. Only spring cured those who survived. The Natives traded fresh meat and green shoots that were devoured by the settlers. Champlain was so curious that he dissected some of the bodies of the dead, only to find that their organs were in a terrible state. In 1535 Jacques Cartier cut white cedar and boiled the bark to cure scurvy.

This plaque in Québec's Lower Town honours Sieur de Mons who was named Lieutenant General of New France by King Henri IV in 1603. He was given the task of founding the colonies in Port Royal and later in Québec. Champlain assisted him in both of these colonies that successfully established French settlement and the French language in North America.

If you crossed the St. Lawrence River now, this is what you would see from the Lower Town.

Spring brought back warmth and health and new growth. That spring I had a new adventure. Some years ago I promised the Montagnais that I would help them against their enemies, the Iroquois. I had a shallop fitted out with everything necessary to carry our explorations south to the country of the Iroquois. Travelling upriver toward Hochelaga we met two or three hundred Montagnais and Hurons encamped on Eloi Island. I talked with their chiefs, Iroquet and Ochastequin, and later they came to my shallop with gifts of furs and showing many signs of pleasure. Many other followers had never seen white men before, so they requested that we return to Québec and show them how we lived. This I agreed to. We set out together for our settlement where they enjoyed themselves dancing and feasting for nearly a week. At the end of June we all went on the warpath.

We travelled upriver to the Richelieu River where we turned south. At the St. Louis rapids [at Chambly] we could go no further with the shallop. I decided to embark with the Natives in their canoes. I was prepared to go alone, if necessary, to prove my promise to my Native allies, but two of my companions were eager to come also. We portaged around the rapids and shortly entered a fine large lake that I called Champlain. We proceeded past islands and beside the mountains until the lake narrowed at Ticonderoga. From there on we travelled by night and hid during the day because we were well into Iroquois country.

This shallop boat is from Champlain's drawing of a battle at an Iroquois fort in New York State.

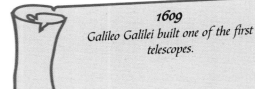

1609
Galileo Galilei built one of the first telescopes.

1611
King James I version of the Bible was published. It is still used today.

1619
The first slaves were brought to Virginia from West Africa.

We met the Iroquois July 29 and all uttered loud shouts and got arms ready. The chiefs agreed to attack at sunrise. Each of us Frenchmen was armed with an arquebus (old style musket), and light armour. The Iroquois came to meet us, two hundred strong, robust men. I admired the gravity and calm with which they came to meet us. Their three chiefs were wearing plumes on their heads. I advanced but was hidden between two groups of warriors. When the opponents saw me they stopped. When I saw them make a move to draw their bows, I raised my gun and shot directly at the chiefs. Two of them died immediately and the other died later in the day. One of my companions, hidden in the woods, fired while I was reloading. The Iroquois, seeing their chiefs dead, lost courage and took flight.

Champlain's Drawing of the Battle at Lake Champlain

1620
The Pilgrim Fathers sailed on the "Mayflower" and settled in Plymouth, Mass.

1620
The first record of a merry-go-round (Turkey)

1621
The first fairy tale, "The History of Tom Thumb the Little", was published in England.

Our allies took ten or twelve prisoners and fifteen of them were wounded, but healed quickly. After gaining our victory, the warriors took a large quantity of Indian corn and shields that the Iroquois had left. The Natives were well pleased with the outcome of the skirmish. After three hours of feasting and dancing we travelled back across the lake and down the Richelieu to the St. Lawrence River. The Hurons and the Algonquins went west and I went east to Québec with the Montagnais.

Champlain Taking an Observation with the Astrolabe on the Ottawa River, 1613

Travels to Lake Huron - 1615

We left Québec to go to the country of the Huron with my interpreter and servant, Thomas Godefroy, Etienne Brûlé and ten Natives in canoes heavily laden with clothing and other supplies. I was much interested in seeing and mapping the great inland seas that I had heard about in many stories. [Champlain entered Lake Nipissing at the site of present day North Bay] At Lake Nipissing we stayed with the Nipissing tribe in their lodges. They were very kind and hospitable to us. They went hunting and fishing in order to entertain us as well as they could. There were about eight hundred people in the area, on the shores and on the pretty islands in the lake.

In May 1613, Champlain travelled up the Ottawa River. To avoid the rapids, he chose a course through a number of small lakes near Cobden, Ontario. Champlain and his men were forced to portage and to climb over and under fallen logs at one difficult point by Green Lake, now known as Astrolabe Lake. It was here that it is believed that Champlain lost the astrolabe. It was not found until 1867, 254 years later when a 14-year-old farm boy named Edward Lee found it while helping his father clear trees. A steamboat captain named Crowley offered Edward ten dollars for the astrolabe. Crowley sold it to his employer, R.W. Cassels of Toronto, but never paid Edward as he had promised. The astrolabe was eventually willed to the New York Historical Society in 1942 where it stayed until 1989, when it was acquired by the Canadian Museum of Civilization. It is on display there now.

Having rested for two days we continued on our way along the French River. The country was full of rocks and not good for farming of any sort. If it were not for an abundance of raspberries and blueberries we would have been hungry. (Champlain called blueberries, bleuets. In Québec, they are still called bleuets today.) We met three hundred men of a tribe called the Cheveux Relevées or high hairs, because they wear their hair arranged very high and better than our courtiers in France.

They had patterns carved on their bodies, painted their faces with different colours, had their noses pierced and their ears fringed with beads. They were in this area to gather blueberries to dry for the winter. After this friendly meeting, we continued down the river and entered Lake Huron. There were many islands at the mouth of the river and fish, such as pike and sturgeon, were plentiful. The land here is very suitable for farming. I went to look at their Indian corn which was far advanced for the season. I stayed in a village called Carhagonha [2 miles from Thunder Bay on Georgian Bay], which was enclosed for defense and protection by a triple wooden palisade thirty-five feet high. Father Joseph lived here. (The first Christian Mission was established in 1615 when four Récollets priests arrived before Champlain's voyage.) We were very glad to see each other again. On August second, the Reverend Father celebrated the Holy Mass and a cross was set up near a little cabin apart from the village. The villagers had built the cabin while I was staying there waiting for the Huron warriors to prepare to go on the warpath against the Iroquois south of the Lake of the Onondagas [Lake Ontario]. These preparations took a very long time.

We set out from Cahiagué on September the first and passed the shore of Lake Couchiching and then Lake Simcoe, which empties into the narrows on the Severn River on its way to Lake Huron. We waited there for more warriors to assemble. Etienne Brûlé went with two canoes of Hurons who were going to rendezvous with the Andastes allies to the south.

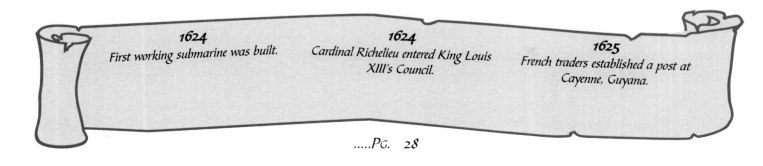

1624
First working submarine was built.

1624
Cardinal Richelieu entered King Louis XIII's Council.

1625
French traders established a post at Cayenne, Guyana.

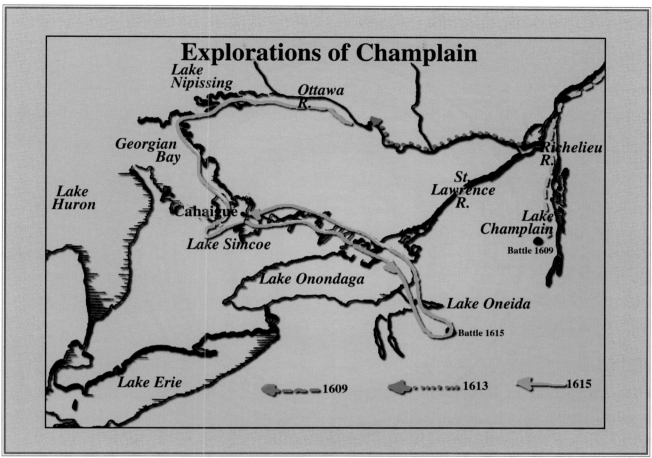

Explorations of Champlain

Lake Nipissing

Ottawa R.

Georgian Bay

Lake Huron

Richelieu R.

St. Lawrence R.

Cahaigue

Lake Champlain

Lake Simcoe

Battle 1609

Lake Onondaga

Lake Oneida

Battle 1615

Lake Erie

1609   1613   1615

We set out again on September 10 and travelled through a series of lakes and rivers [the Trent River system, Sturgeon Lake, Balsam Lake], to the Lake of the Onondagas [Lake Ontario]. We crossed the lake and entered enemy country. The Hurons hid their canoes, then we went on foot along a sandy beach [Henderson Bay, New York]. During the four days' journey we crossed a number of streams and a river [the Oneida]. On the ninth of October our men went out scouting and captured eleven Iroquois while they were fishing.

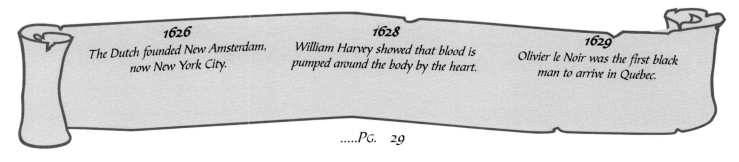

1626
The Dutch founded New Amsterdam, now New York City.

1628
William Harvey showed that blood is pumped around the body by the heart.

1629
Olivier le Noir was the first black man to arrive in Québec.

The next day we arrived at the Iroquois fort [near Lake Onondaga]. There was a small skirmish which ended when we fired the arquebuses. The Iroquois retreated. I instructed the Hurons in building a cavalier from which five arquebuses could fire into the Iroquois compound. We were awaiting the arrival of five hundred warriors of the Andastes tribe, along with Brûlé and the Huron warriors. Seeing that the Iroquois were further fortifying their palisades, I counselled that we should not wait but follow our plan of attack. The battle went well for a time and then some of the Hurons set a fire against the palisade in the wrong place. The Iroquois extinguished it easily. There was utter confusion so that my orders could not be heard. Some of the Huron leaders were wounded and the warriors lost heart and retreated. The chiefs have no absolute control over their men, who follow their own wishes when they choose, so disorderly retreats are common. We withdrew to our fort to treat the wounded before we set out on our trek back to the canoes.

Huron Woman and
Warrior
by Champlain

Cheveux Relevées
(later called Ottawa)

Champlain describes them as hunters, warriors and fishermen. They were the cleanest in their household affairs, industrious in making mats, which were their Turkey carpets. They were great people for feasts, more than other tribes.

I sustained two wounds, one in the leg and the other in the knee, which gave me great pain. This was nothing compared to the pain I experienced while being carried on the back of one of the warriors because I could not stand. As soon as I had gained strength enough to stand, I did so to get out of that hellish prison on the man's back.

When we arrived back at the Lake of the Onondagas, we were relieved to find our canoes intact. I begged the Hurons to take me back to Québec, but they would not, so I travelled with them back to their country. We hunted and waited for the rivers to freeze so that travelling would be easier. The Hurons made a travois (sled) to pull on the ice to carry their belongings. On December 23 we reached Cahiagué. Once rested, I set out to see Father Joseph and during the winter we visited seven other villages. We were greeted with good cheer, gifts of meat and fish and friendly feeling.

A PALISADED HURON-IROQUOIS VILLAGE

The Huron

The Huron and their close relatives, the Tobacco Huron, lived in Ontario between Lake Simcoe and Georgian Bay. In 1600, they were estimated to have had a population of 20,000 people. They lived in towns and villages protected by palisades. The houses were arranged in regular rows along streets but far enough apart to prevent the spread of fire. Cahiagué, one of the largest towns, had a population of between 4,000 and 6,000 people and over two hundred longhouses. Longhouses were 50-60m long, 12m wide and 8m high. The frames were made of poles from trees and the exterior was covered with slabs of bark. Each house was divided into compartments for families related through the mother's line. The house was shared by at least ten family units.

During this time I was asked by the Nipissings to come and speak with Chief Iroquet to help settle a dispute between his tribe and the Hurons. This I was happy to do because as guests of the Hurons, we, the French, could find ourselves in an awkward and dangerous position if the dispute continued between these tribes. I begged them not to call upon me to effect this agreement if they did not intend to follow, point by point, the advice I should give them. It was in their best interests to resolve their differences because united, they might more easily resist their enemies. After much talk and conditions that were agreeable to both sides, the negotiations were successful. For the remainder of the winter season, which lasted four months, I had the leisure to study their country, modes of life and the form of their assemblies.

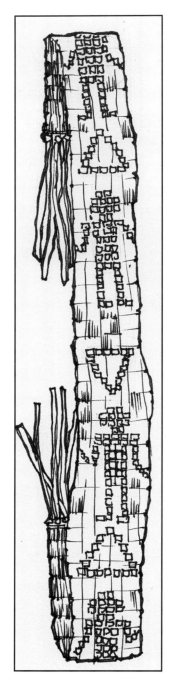

This belt shows some of the symbols used in wampum belts. The Iroquois used tiny beads made from sea shells to fashion wampum belts. They had a rich oral tradition but no written language, so they used the symbols woven into the belts to remind them of past events. In their dealings with the Europeans, agreements were made and then the terms of the pact were woven into a belt.

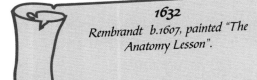

1632
Rembrandt b.1607, painted "The Anatomy Lesson".

1635
First printing press in America set up in Massachusetts

1636
Connecticut was settled.

Women Described by Champlain

They wore robes with a belt at the waist. They were laden with quantities of wampum (shell beads), both necklaces and chains which hung down in front of their robes and were attached to their belts. They had their hair well-combed, dyed and oiled and they went to dances with a tuft of their hair behind, tied up with eel-skin. In this manner, gaily adorned, they liked to show themselves at festivities. They were strong and robust. A good number were pretty and pleasing both in figure, complexion and with features all in harmony. There were also powerful women of extraordinary stature, for it is they who cared for the house and did the work. They tilled the soil, stripped the hemp and spun it, made fish nets, harvested corn, stored it, prepared food and carried the baggage. The men hunt, fish, build lodges and go on the war-path.

Huron People Harvesting Corn

The Huron carried their babies on a decorated cradleboard similar to this one.

The Children Described by Champlain

The Huron placed a small child, in the daytime, on a small wooden board and clothed and wrapped it in furs and tied it to the board, which stood upright. They also put under the child a bed of down from cat-tails and they cleaned them with the same down. To adorn the child, they decked the board with beads and put some beads around its neck, no matter how small the baby was. Babies slept between their mother and father at night. The children had great freedom among these tribes; the parents humoured them too much and punished them not at all.

1637
The Japanese were the first to blow their noses on paper tissues.

1638-1715
Louis XIV "The Sun King"

1642-1727
Scientist Sir Isaac Newton

We set out for Québec on May 20, 1616. The trip took forty days. De Monts met us and was very happy to see us because he had heard rumours that we were dead. I bade our Huron guides farewell and said I would visit them in the future to assist them as I had done in the past. I was heartened to find that our first woman settler, Marguerite Vienne, had arrived. She ministered to the needs of the ill settlers and workers in the settlement. Encouraged by her, I recruited settlers while I was back in France during the winter of 1617. My old friend, Louis Hébert, the pharmacist from Port Royal, came to Québec with his wife, two daughters and one son. They became the first farming family in Québec. A year later, one of Louis's daughters married a colonist.

Champlain leaves Québec as a prisoner on Kirke's ship in 1629.

In 1620, I brought my wife, Hélène, to New France. I named an Island, Ile Ste. Hélène after her. I had brought Iroquet's son, Savignon, to France to tell her about New France. I was distressed when I saw the condition of the Habitation at Québec.

It looked like some poor house abandoned in the fields after being used by soldiers. I quickly ordered and organized the repairs, but it took some time before it was comfortable. Unfortunately, Hélène never got used to life in this new country. She was gracious and kind to our Native friends. She wore a mirrored pendant as a necklace. One day a Native woman asked Hélène why she could see her face on Hélène. She replied, "Because you are always in my heart." Hélène and I returned to France in 1624.

The Statue of Samuel de Champlain in Québec City

Champlain returned to Québec only to see it overthrown by the English in 1629. Québec was handed back to France in 1632 in the Treaty of St. Germaine-en-Laye. The settlement had deteriorated in every way. The English, under Kirke, had traded whisky and firearms to the Natives for furs, with disastrous results.

Champlain stayed on in Québec administering the small colony of only 300 people as the king's representative for France, until he took ill in the fall of 1635 and was paralyzed. He had a stroke on Christmas Day in 1635, exactly one hundred years after Jacques Cartier's first Christmas in Québec.

Conclusion

Edward Gaylord Bourne, Professor of History at Yale University said, in 1906, that Champlain was the founder of New France and chief of its early historians. A leader of indefatigable energy and sterling character; a Frenchman who devoted his life to extending the name and power of France and the civilizing influences of the Church. Although we have no physical likeness of the man, his moral image is indelibly stamped on the memory of every student of his writings. He had a singularly well-rounded character, full of strength and dignity and sweetness, compared with other explorers and founders of that age. He stands above them in the range of his achievements of permanent positive contribution to knowledge, of bringing order out of chaos to North American cartography and his sympathetic observations of Native life.

Glossary

cavalier: a structure built with a platform higher than the palisade surrounding an enemy village so that warriors could shoot muskets and arrows into the Native village

civil: showing civilization; not barbarous

cordial: warm, hearty, sincere, and friendly

courtiers: people attending royal court

emaciated: extremely thin due to starvation

famine: extreme scarcity of food; starvation

fraught: filled; laden

Hochelaga: the original name for Montréal

indefatigable: tireless

indelibly: marked permanently; unable to be erased

Inquisition: an agency in the Catholic Church formed to seek out non-believers and punish them. The Spanish Inquisition was very severe.

myriad: a very large number; countless

predisposition: a tendency towards a person or a thing

sentinel: a soldier who stands guard

sterling: of solid worth; not showy

trek: a slow, difficult journey

More to Do

Books...Fiction for Young People

Aubry, Claude. AGOUHANNA. Toronto: Doubleday, 1993.
How did the Iroquois live before white people arrived in North America?

Boyd, David. CHAMPLAIN SUMMER. Oakville: Rubicon Publishing, 1993.
While doing a school project on Champlain, a boy finds traces of the great explorer.

Bruchac, Joseph. CHILDREN OF THE LONG-HOUSE. New York: Dial, 1986.
An exciting story set in a Mohawk village around 1490.

Cook, Lyn. THE HIDING PLACE. Toronto: Stoddart, 1996.
In 1650 in New France, Monsieur Gaudin wants to marry 12 year old Justine. Her brother and a Native boy help her escape.

Katz, Welwyn Wilton. FALSE FACE. Vancouver: Douglas and McIntyre, 1987.
Two teens discover Iroquois face masks in a bog and soon learn that these ancient artifacts are powerful.

Books...Non-fiction for Young People

Bowers, Vivien. WOW CANADA! Exploring This Land From Coast to Coast. Toronto: Owl Books, 1999.

Coulter, Tony. JACQUES CARTIER, SAMUEL de CHAMPLAIN AND THE EXPLORERS OF CANADA. New York: Chelsea House Publishers, 1993.

Doherty, Craig and Katherine Doherty. THE IROQUOIS. Franklin Watts, 1991.

Jacobs, William Jay. CHAMPLAIN: A LIFE OF COURAGE. New York: Franklin Watts, 1994.

Legay, Gilbert. ATLAS OF INDIANS OF NORTH AMERICA. New York: Barron's Publishers, 1995.

Livesay, Robert and A.G. Smith. DISCOVERING CANADA: NATIVE PEOPLES. Toronto: Stoddart, 1993.

Livesay, Robert and A.G. Smith. DISCOVERING CANADA: NEW FRANCE. Toronto: Stoddart, 1990.

Lunn, Janet and Christopher Moore. THE STORY OF CANADA. Toronto: Lester Publishing and Key Porter Books, 1992.

Owens, Ann-Maureen and Jane Yealland. FORTS OF CANADA. Toronto: Kids Can Press, 1998.

Tolhurst, Marilyn. EXPLORERS HANDBOOK: How to Become a Fearless Adventurer. Richmond Hill: Scholastic Canada, 1998.

Web Sites

Web Sites

Archaeology of an Iroquoian Longhouse
www.rom.on.ca/digs/longhouse
Explore an archaeological site and a village as it might have been.

National Atlas of Canada Online
www.atlas.gc.ca
Learn about Canada's geography.

Seed-Barker Site
www.rom.on.ca/digs/seedbarker/
Excavation of an Iroquoian site north of Toronto in 1997.

Virtual Museum of New France
www.vmnf.civilization.ca/
Learn about French explorers and life in New France.

Places to Visit

Nova Scotia

Port Royal National Historic Site - The Habitation
P.O. Box 9, Annapolis Royal, N.S. B0S 1A0
902-532-2898. www.parkscanada.pch.gc.ca
Discover the trials and the successes of the colonists who settled this area.

Québec

Canadian Museum of Civilization,
Hull, 1-800-555-5621. www.civilization.ca
Illustrates Canada's history from prehistoric to modern times, including exploration, the fur trade and Champlain's astrolabe.

Festival of New France
Québec City, www.nouvellefrance.qc.ca
Held annually in early August to celebrate the French Regime during the 17th and 18th centuries.

Québec City Historic District
www.quebecregion.com
A UNESCO World Heritage Site. Wander the historic streets of Quartier Petit-Champlain and visit Place-Royale

Kahnawake Tourism Information Centre
Near Montreal, 450-638-9699
A unique village where you can experience traditional Mohawk music, food and arts.

Musée du Fort Stewart
Ile Ste. Hélène, Montréal
514-861-6701. www.stewart-museum.org
Military artifacts, maps and models from the early days of Canada.

Parc Archéologique de la Pointe du Buisson,
Melocheville, 450-429-7857
Abundant evidence found here that people camped and worked here beginning about 5000 years ago. Participate outdoors or in the laboratory.

Ontario

Anishinabe Experience
Golden Lake (near Pembroke)
613-625-2519. anishexp@renc.igs.net
Experience Algonquin First Nation storytelling, cooking, and accommodation in teepees.

Crawford Lake Conservation Area
2596 Britannia Rd. W., R.R. 2
Milton, L9T 2X6.
905-854-0234. crawlake@hrca.on.ca
Site of an important precontact Iroquoian village with several reconstructed longhouses. Many special programmes and events.

Etienne Brûlé Park and Toronto Carrying Place
Toronto
A city park on the Humber River commemorating the historic canoe route between Lakes Simcoe and Ontario.

Huronia Museum and Huron Indian Villages
Midland, L4R 4P4.
705-526-2844. hmchin@bconnex.net
www.georgianbaytourism.on.ca
Contains Native and European material from over 40 archaeological excavations in Ontario.

Champlain Monument by Vernon March
Couchiching Beach Park, Orillia.
One of the finest bronzes on the continent.

Statue of Champlain by Hamilton MacCarthy
Nepean Point, Ottawa.

Petroglyphs Provincial Park
N-E of Peterborough, G.D. Woodview, K0L 3E0
705-877-2552. www.ontarioparks.com
900 petroglyphs carved in marble seem to have been created between 500 and 1000 years ago by Algonquin people.

Samuel de Champlain Provincial Park
Near Mattawa.
705-744-2276. www.ontarioparks.com
The Voyageur Heritage Centre pays tribute to the famous explorer and voyageurs with exhibits including a huge bark canoe.

Woodland Cultural Centre
Brantford.
519-759-2650. www.woodland-centre.on.ca
Exhibits relating to the First Nations People of the eastern woodlands.

Bibliography

Armstrong, Joe C. W. *CHAMPLAIN*. Toronto: MacMillan, 1987.

Brown, Craig (editor). *THE ILLUSTRATED HISTORY OF CANADA*. Toronto: Lester Publishing, 1996.

Champlain, Samuel de. *DES SAUVAGES (1603)*. The Champlain Society, Toronto: University of Toronto Press, 1971.

Champlain, Samuel de. *VOYAGES DU SIEUR de CHAMPLAIN (1613)*. The Champlain Society, Toronto: University of Toronto Press, 1971.

Champlain, Samuel de. *VOYAGES (1632)*. The Champlain Society, Toronto: University of Toronto Press, 1971.

Colby, Charles W. *FOUNDER OF NEW FRANCE - A CHRONICLE OF CHAMPLAIN*. Toronto: University of Toronto Press, 1964.

Costain, Thomas B. *THE WHITE AND THE GOLD*. Garden City: Doubleday, 1954.

Edwards, Cecile Pepin. *CHAMPLAIN, FATHER OF NEW FRANCE*. New York: Abingdon, 1955.

Garrod, Stan. *SAMUEL de CHAMPLAIN*. Markham: Fitzhenry and Whiteside, 1981.

Garrod, Stan. *VOYAGES OF DISCOVERY*. Markham: Fitzhenry and Whiteside, 1985.

Hannon, Leslie F. *THE DISCOVERERS*. Toronto: McClelland and Stewart, 1971.

Jefferys, Charles W. *PICTURE GALLERY OF CANADIAN HISTORY, Vol. I*. Toronto: Ryerson Press, 1963.

Jenness, Diamond. *INDIANS OF CANADA*. Toronto: University of Toronto Press, 1977.

Jones, Colin. *CAMBRIDGE ILLUSTRATED HISTORY OF FRANCE*. Cambridge: Cambridge University Press, 1994.

Jones, Elizabeth. *GENTLEMEN AND JESUITS*. Toronto: University of Toronto Press, 1986.

Lescarbot, Marc. *HISTOIRE de la NOUVELLE FRANCE (1609)* in three volumes. Toronto: Champlain Society, 1907-14.

Macklem, Michael. (translator). *SAMUEL de CHAMPLAIN: VOYAGES TO NEW FRANCE, 1599-1603*. Canada: Oberon Press, 1971.

Muchembled, Robert. *POPULAR CULTURE AND ELITE CULTURE IN FRANCE 1400-1750*. Baton Rouge: Louisiana State University Press, 1985.

Tait, George E. *BREASTPLATE AND BUCKSKIN*. Toronto: Ryerson Press, 1953.

Tanner, Helen Hornbeck. *ATLAS OF GREAT LAKES INDIAN HISTORY*. University of Oklahoma: Norman, 1987.

THE VOYAGES OF EXPLORATION OF SAMUEL de CHAMPLAIN (1604-1616) Vol. I. Toronto: Courier Press, 1911.

Time-Life Books. *REALM OF THE IROQUOIS*. Alexandria, Virginia: Time-Life Books, 1993.

Wright, Ronald. *STOLEN CONTINENTS*. Toronto: Penguin, 1992.

Picture Credits

Index

Algonquin 10, 22, 23, 26, 32
arquebus 25, 30
astrolabe 26, 27

Bible 24
blueberries 27
Brouage 5
Brûlé, Etienne 27, 28, 30

Cacao (hot chocolate) 6
canoe 11, 22, 24, 27, 29, 31
Cardinal Richelieu 28
Cartier, Jacques 23, 35
Champlain and St. Lawrence Railroad 20
Cheveux Relevées 27, 30
Cochineal 20
Connecticut 32
Cuba 8

D'Acosta, Mathew 13, 16
de Biencourt, Jean, Seigneur de Poutrincourt
13, 15, 16, 17
Drake, Sir Francis 10
Duval, Jean 18, 19

Edict of Nantes 4

Fairy tale 25
Father Joseph 28, 31
France 10, 12, 14, 17, 19, 27, 35
Frobisher, Sir Martin 10
fur trade 9, 35

Galileo 24
Gunpowder Plot 15

Habitation 13, 15, 18, 23, 34
heart 29
Hébert, Louis 13, 16, 34
Hélène 34, 35
Hochelaga 24
Hudson, Henry 18
Huron 22, 24, 28, 29, 30, 31, 32, 33, 34

Indies 5, 8
Inquisition 8,
Iroquois 7, 10, 12, 22, 23, 24, 25, 26, 28, 29, 30
Ivan the Terrible 6

Kepler, Johan 19
King Henri IV (1589-1610) 9, 10, 13, 17, 18
King Lear 15
King of Spain 5, 6, 8

Lake Huron 27, 28
Lake of the Onondagas 28, 29, 30, 31
Lescarbot, Marc 13, 17
Louis XIV 33

mapping 5, 7, 27
Memberton 16, 17
merry-go-round 25
Mexico (New Spain) 6, 7,
Mi'kmaq 16, 17
Montagnais 9, 10, 22, 23, 24, 26, 32
Montréal 11

Natal, Antoine 18
Native 8, 9, 10, 12, 23, 27
Neptune 15, 16, 17
New Amsterdam 29
New Brunswick 13
New France 5, 8, 9, 12, 34, 35
Newton, Sir Isaac 33
Nipissing 32
Nova Scotia 12, 13, 15, 17

Order of Good Cheer 16, 17
Orient 8, 11

Pilgrim Fathers 25
Pocahontas 19
Pont-Gravé, François 9, 10, 11, 13, 19
Porto Rico 5, 6,
Port Royal 13, 14, 15, 16, 17, 34
printing press 32

Québec 18, 22, 24, 26, 27, 31, 34, 35
Queen Elizabeth I 14

Raleigh, Sir Walter 11
Rembrandt 18, 32
Richelieu River 10, 24, 26

Sagamo 9, 15, 16
scurvy 16, 22, 23
Shakespeare, William 6
shallop 11, 24
Sieur de Monts 13, 17, 23, 34
slaves 24
Smith, John 19
Spanish armada 11
St. Lawrence River 9, 12, 18, 26
St. Peter's Cathedral 11
submarine 28

Tadoussac 9, 10, 11
Three Blind Mice 19
Ticonderoga 24, 25
Trois Rivières 12

wampum 32, 33